7 Ways to Win Political Debates with Your Liberal Family and Friends.

And still keep them as family and friends.

By Rusty Humphries

Rusty Humphries
Anthem, Arizona 85086
E-mail: Rusty@RustyLive.com

Limits of Liability and Disclaimer of Warranty
The author and publisher shall not be liable for your misuse of this material. This book is intended for use by conservatives only, and is to be used for the purpose of good, not evil. This book is for strictly informational and educational purposes.

Disclaimer
The views expressed are those of the author, and they are correct. Anyone who disagrees with author is wrong! Personal stories told by the author are almost 100% accurate and truthful. Even if you follow the tips and you still manage to get into a political battle, or lose the love of a family member or friend, it's not the author's fault. Take responsibility of your life, Snowflake. These are ideas and tips, not Executive Orders written by Obama, which must be followed without question in perpetuity. Image of Ed Rush in a flight suit was taken with a suit bought at the owner's expense, so back off!

Copyright Use and Public Information
Unless otherwise noted, images have been used by permission and are in keeping with public information laws. Please contact the author for questions about copyrights or the use of public information. Used by permission. All rights reserved.

Be the "Go-To" Celebrity in your niche market!
"America's Media Talent Coach" Rusty Humphries
has limited openings for VIP Coaching programs.
Find out more at www.RustyLive.com.

Find out more about Rusty Humphries at RustyLive.com.
The Rusty Humphries Rebellion is available on
iTunes, iHeartRadio, and Stitcher.
Please LIKE and follow him on Facebook
https://www.facebook.com/Talk2Rusty/
and @Talk2Rusty on Twitter.

CELEBRITY ENDORSEMENTS FOR RUSTY HUMPHRIES

I've been in more political debates than I care to remember. I wish I had this book a few years ago. I've worked with Rusty Humphries, he's incredible, I LOVE him!

It's true, Rusty Humphries IS "America's Media Talent Coach."

Stacey Dash

Actress *Clueless*,

Author *There Goes My Social Life: From Clueless to Conservative*

Fighting with a liberal can be very complicated, as they usually do not base their opinion on reality or fact. Rusty Humphries taught me how to connect the dots of my arguments in order to form the trap, which ultimately exposes the ignorance or hypocrisy of my opponent's argument.

Scottie Nell Hughes

Former Trump Surrogate

Seen on FOX NEWS/CNN/MSNBC and many, many more.

Author *ROAR - The New Conservative Woman Speaks Out*

Spokeswoman for The Committee to Defend the President

Rusty Humphries' new book is a textbook on debating the left.

Read it now and become a better fighter for the cause.

Ben Shapiro

Author *Bullies: How the Left's Culture of Fear and Intimidation Silences Americans*

Editor in chief of the Daily Wire

I've written material for presidential candidates, and the best of the best at the highest levels of show business. Nobody has a better complete working knowledge of media, combined with the gift of teaching, like Rusty Humphries, nobody!

Evan Sayet

Comedian

Author *KinderGarden Of Eden: How the Modern Liberal Thinks*

TABLE OF CONTENTS

FOREWORD BY ED RUSH – FIGHTER PILOT

It was Thanksgiving 1992, with the standard cast of characters. The problem with Thanksgiving (and the standard cast of characters) is you're pretty much stuck with who you've got. The only way to change the lineup and swing the balance was through marriage, and back in 1992, I wasn't ready for that yet.

So, there I sat at Thanksgiving dinner surrounded by an unholy mix of conservative, liberal, and *stupid*.

To make matters worse, the presidential election of George W. Bush and Bill Clinton was right around the corner.

Sitting at the table slopping her turkey and stuffing was Aunt Fergie. You know that one family member that pretty much "doesn't get it?" Yeah. That's Aunt Fergie. Inevitably, the conversation shifted to politics. That's precisely the moment Aunt Fergie came up for air to state, *"I am voting for the Clinton. I really like him."*

To which I (a stalwart Bush voter) simply asked, *"What is it you like so much about him, Aunt Fergie?"*

Two more scoops of imitation mashed potatoes and then a quick reply, *"I think what we really need is change."*

To which I (a now even more stalwart Bush voter) replied, *"What, specifically, do you want to change?"*

Fergie stopped, spoon dripping gravy, and stared for what seemed like an hour. Her eyes shifted. Breath waned. And then, with the renewed vigor of a prize fighter coming off the ropes, she confidently and proudly declared, *"It's just that... things have to CHANGE!"*

My first lesson in the world of family politics.

If only I had Rusty Humphries' book back in 1992, I would have been able to move through the dinner with deft and elo-

quence. I would have picked my battles, kept my family close, been the reasonable one, engaged, and even been okay losing. As it was, I lost my mind and still remember the conversation vividly so many years later.

Learn from my mistake, and study this book like your life depends on it. Plus, you're going to love this book. It's fun, funny, and it's a solid primer on how to hold your ground without losing your friends. Until this book, I was under the misconception that I could either honor the *relationship* or be *right*.

Now, I know I can have both.

Ed Rush

Fighter Pilot, 4-Time Best Selling Author

Personal Friend of Rusty Humphries

EdRush.com

ACKNOWLEDGMENTS

I'm a talk show host, not a writer. My friend, Orson Scott Card, now that guy is a writer! I write like I talk: loud, brash, and with my tongue firmly planted in my cheek at all times. There is a lot of serious info in this book, but if you think it's going to be all serious, HA!

As a warning, if you are a member of the grammar police, you might as well pull out your ticket book and start writing me up now. I acknowledge this book isn't perfectly grammatical and it's totally my fault. I hereby release Mr. Kelly, my 10th and 11th grade English teacher, from any and all blame. And, I apologize to my incredibly awesome (and good lookin') editor, Janille Baxter, who worked hours and hours of overtime fixing my "issues."

Did you know there are different style guides for columns and books? Ya, me neither, ugh... rules, rules, and more rules. I hate rules; I'm a rule breaker! To quote the great philosopher Pee-Wee Herman, from 1985's classic movie *Pee-wee's Big Adventure*, "I'm a loner, Dottie. A rebel."

Thankfully for you, Janille was able to fix a lot of my sloppy writing. But don't worry, I read it my way in the audiobook version the way the good Lord intended: sloppy, with lots of asides thrown in, and full of grammatical errors. Either way, enjoy this publication; you will learn a lot of cool stuff.

So, please sit back and enjoy my ramblings.

Oh ya... I'm supposed to thank people in this section; it's one of the rules!

Thank you to my parents for being there and who lent me money when I needed it. Thank you to me, for not spending that money on smack, hookers, or blow. Thank you, Mark Young, for your unwavering support and friendship. Thank you, Chuck Woolery, you're not just the best game show host ever, but you're one of the nicest guys ever, too. Thank you, Mark Muller, for teaching me to be a real man, even though I am far superior when it comes to the art of BBQ. Thank you, Ed Rush and Mike Koenigs, for your help in my career transition. Thank you, Mike Hawkins and Tiffiny Ruegner at Right Wing News, for allowing me to be a part of your fantastic team.

Thank you to my VIP media talent clients, keep up the great work. I'm so proud of you. (Yes, you can get a book for free.)

THANK YOU: Stacey Dash, Scottie Nell Hughes, Walter Sabo, Ben Shapiro, Dr. Gina Loudon, Rep. Michele Bachmann, Ken "Spanky" Moskowitz, Kathleen Kennedy, Doug and Nancy Baxter, Orson Scott Card, Lisa Marie Wark, Steve Gill, Even Sayet, Ross Shafer, Margaret Howell, Christopher Masters, Uncle Ted Nugent, David Sweeney, and Rick Allen.

Presidential little brother, Roger Clinton, thank you for being one of those guys I can debate, hang out with, and like, even though you're a Democrat. :)

To my beautiful radio, podcast and online audience, you really are my friends. I can't tell you how much your support has meant to my family and me over the years. It sounds a bit hokey saying, but, really, "I couldn't have done it without you." Thank you very, very, much!

To my two beautiful, brilliant and wonderful daughters, Karaline and Katelynn. Thank you for not giving up on me. I know it's hard when your Dad is traveling the country giving speeches to strangers. Thank you for understanding. I pray you know deep in your hearts, that I wished I were home with you when I was away. Never forget, I'm working with a lot of my friends, to save our country. I do this not for my self-worth, but so you and your future children will have a country you can be proud of, believe in and love, as much as I do. I love you both very much.

And now, on with the show!

INTRODUCTION

Those who know, don't talk. Those who talk, don't know.

— Lao Tzu, ancient Chinese philosopher 604 BC – 531 BC

Almost every day I receive a phone call or an email, or I meet someone on the street, who says, "I've got a sister (brother, cousin, sister-in-law…), who is a big liberal. I love her, but every time we have a family get-together, there's a big fight. What do I do?"

My friend, this book is the answer to your prayers and will answer all your questions.

However, if you're looking to go headfirst into serious political debates, battling it out with every snowflake, Chick-fil-A hater, and President Donald Trump derangement sufferer, you might want to look for another title. (Although this book will point you in the right direction.) This is a book to help you deal with your family and friends in the most dangerous of all arenas of battle, social situations.

If you are a liberal and you're reading this book to find ways to defeat a conservative…

Stop!

I repeat, STOP!

I've written this book with the express intent of helping my conservative brothers and sisters keep the family and friends they haven't lost just because they voted for President Donald J. Trump.

This book is not intended to help liberals in any way other than to calm them down.

I caution you, you must use these techniques for good. Like the unearthed tomb of a pharaoh, I place a curse on anyone who uses these words and tips for evil. I do not wish to lose my blessings from the Lord.

Let's Make American Families Great Again! We need each other.

Rusty Humphries
June 2017

As a top-rated radio and TV talk show host for nearly 30 years, I've had more than my share of political debates. I have participated in literally thousands of them. Dealing with people on the left can be frustrating and sometimes downright impossible. Thankfully, I've always had an advantage; I'm in control of the show and in control of the microphone. I'll be honest, it's fun to have the power to hang up on any caller or guest anytime I want. That makes for an interesting and entertaining radio show. My problem hasn't been in dealing with the Left on radio or TV; it's been the attacks in my personal life, which have given me the most heartache.

At times, it's made me feel antisocial, not wanting to go out and meet with people. Not because I'm a hermit or don't like "the folks". It's because two phenomena happen almost every time I'm introduced to someone new.

#1 I meet a person/s who shares my conservative values. They're nice, very intelligent, usually have heard my radio show, have seen me on Fox News, or seen my materials online. The discussion often quickly turns to politics, and while they are well-intentioned, it makes me feel like I have to perform my radio show for them live, instead of having a pleasant evening. People tend to forget that I have other likes, hobbies, and interests outside of the political world. I've come to the realization, though, these people are well-meaning, and for them, sometimes it's just nice to be able to talk to somebody else who agrees with you. I get that.

#2 As soon as someone who can't get enough of Rachel Maddow finds out I'm a radio talk show host, they hunt me down like an up-and-coming gunfighter looking to take on Billy the Kid. It's not just that they're looking for a fight; they're looking to feel important. They want to get back at someone because they feel like somebody done them wrong. It's not about debate, and it's not about finding the best solution for America. It's just about them winning and the other person losing.

Those people drive me crazy. I can't stand them! They approach me with a smirk of righteous disgust. They project an attitude that says, "I'm superior, and I'm here to teach you a lesson." They are bullies, and bullies deserve to be punished.

Let me make something crystal clear: I do not go out looking for a political battle wherever I go. If I'm approached by someone who disagrees with me but is nice and wants to have a genuine, open discussion, I love that; let's talk. I'm all in.

However, the moment one of these douchebags approaches and becomes rude and insulting, it's game on. Here's a warning: If you're a Progressive pinhead looking for puny, political points and you challenge me with your misguided, lack-of-deep-thought, liberal talking points and you think you can keep up? Get ready Gomer—you're going to go down, HARD! It's not hyperbole; it's just a fact. You see, I relish the mental destruction I will rain down upon you. Disrespect me or someone I'm with, and I will make it an evening you will never forget and neither will your friends. Your embarrassment will last a lifetime. For years to come, your friends and loved ones will remember that encounter with me as your greatest moment of shame.

Your so-called friends will celebrate your "Day of Embarrassment" and will gleefully snicker behind your broken, little back. You will have nightmares—horrible, reoccurring nightmares—of how I punished you in front of everyone in the vicinity. Your friends will happily tell everyone you know and they will also laugh at the permanent pain I have caused you.

You will shed tears; my vanquished, pathetic, little challenger and you will most likely consider thoughts of retribution, against my family and me. You will need daily affirmations written by America's worst Senator, Al Franken, repeated ad nauseam: "I'm good enough, I'm smart enough, and doggone it, people like me."

But for me, these trivial foes mean nothing. It's just another debate opponent crushed by the truth, reason, and an understanding of their arguments better than they do. They will wish and dream of a rematch with me for the rest of their lives. They are hoping to regain just a bit of their self-respect. Me? I'll forget about them the moment I walk out of the room... just another sad snowflake melted by my inferno of skill, knowledge, and truth.

That's what happens if I'm out and get verbally assaulted by someone I don't know nor care about.

Unfortunately, that's not how it works when I get together with family and friends. Both phenomena still occur. Either they agree with my point of view and want to talk, or they disagree and want to fight. The question is, how do you keep from turning the family cookout into the family blowout?

Do you have liberal friends and family members who want to debate you every time they see you? Tired of it? Me, too! Want it to stop or beat them every time they get in your face? Good!

This book should cost you a lot, like over $100. It's worth ten times that. Why? Because I have the answers, techniques, and tricks you've been looking for. I'm getting ripped off like a senior citizen chatting online with a Nigerian prince who just wants to transfer $5,000,000 in the kindly Seniors bank account, in exchange for small incidental expenses. What a guy!

I don't mind that you're getting the better of this deal. I like you and I want to help.

If you follow these 7 tips, you will win the argument, look good, and not lose your family and friends.

These may be the most important pages you ever read, ever!

CHAPTER 1

PICK YOUR BATTLES

The perfect battle is the one that does not have to be fought.

—Sun Tzu, Chinese general and philosopher 544 BC – 496 BC

It seems pretty obvious that when you walk into a family or social environment, you don't go in looking for a fight. I wish everyone felt that way, but I can't tell you how many times I have heard from my fellow conservatives that it happens. Every time they see a certain family member, that person is out looking for blood. All they want to do is fight. Could be an in-law, brother, sister, mom, dad, or cousin. Whoever it is, for some reason you push their buttons. For some reason, they think they need to study up and get ready to rumble, just to teach you a lesson. Well my brothers and sisters, we're going to wipe that stupid smile off their face and teach them that this is not the time or place to have these kinds of arguments. You will have everyone in your family know, whether they agree or disagree with you politically, that you are the better man or woman.

It really does start with picking your battles. When some libtard approaches me, and the smell of BO and patchouli oil is strong,

I start playing Michael Jackson's "P.Y.T." in my head. I change the initials to P.Y.B. (Pick your battles.) It's a fun way to remind myself not to engage with someone who is intellectually inferior, and even better… I really like that song.

You have to ask yourself, does the snide comment your family member hurls at you (probably stolen from Stephen Colbert) really require your response? Is the insane verbal attack on President Trump and his supporters really worth taking time away from eating that nice, juicy steak?

I need to share a long, but important story with you. It's a personal, weird, frightening, insane, freaky experience I had a couple of years ago. Study my words and learn young Skywalker and you too can use the force for good, against the force of evil.

First, let me set the stage. I've known my girlfriend since we were in fourth grade. We grew up together, went to the same school and same church, and had many of the same friends. She was the most gorgeous girl in school, and I was the short, fat, mouthy one, so I had absolutely no chance with her. Fast-forward 30 years… we've been together for years, and I win (LOL). I still get Facebook comments and emails from former classmates. "You're with her?! I was totally in love with her back in the day." If they were honest, they would admit, they still have a crush on her. Yes, I'm a lucky man.

Moving along from my bragging. We'll call my girlfriend Bella. She and I have a common friend, Cori, who was her best friend in school, and one night, we were invited to go to dinner with her and her husband, Mike. At that point, everything was great. Then, at the last minute, they told us they invited a friend who really wanted to meet me. (Cue menacing orchestra. Da, Da, da, daaaaaaaaaaaaaa!)

Here's where it gets a little confusing, but I will try to make this as easy as possible to follow. I'm not using real names because I don't want to embarrass my friends, and I don't want a crazy person to try to sue me. Let me tell you about the hag who I call, "Senorita Crazy" — she's my attacker and my nemesis in this book. You will be soon well-acquainted with her — I've changed her name, for the protection of everyone involved. Who knows what she would do, she's nuts. If it went to court, she'd lose. Even thinking about being in the same room with her again gives me the "heebie-jeebies." What am I talking about? Let's continue…

The scene: Sunset at a beautiful lakefront home. We are outside eating dinner around a campfire on the lakeshore. The four of us are enjoying a nice, quiet evening, getting reacquainted with old friends. Then in storms Senorita Crazy (late of course), and while we all brought expensive food and drink to share, she shows up with a single flower for each of us, as a gift. And she's just gushing about how special the flower is. My first thought… uh oh, I've got a bad feeling about this chick.

She sits down and we all start eating, everyone is just enjoying a little small talk, for about three minutes. Then in a voice a little too loud and with a twinge of condescension, Senorita Crazy says, "Rusty, I asked Cori if I could meet you. I'm so very excited to ask you some questions. Just so you know, I'm a very important businesswoman. I make the big bucks, and a number of my employees listen to you on talk radio." (Yes, she actually said, "I'm a very important person, and I make the big bucks." I'm telling you, this is ALL true!)

"That's nice," I say, getting ready for what is about to be flung my way.

"I find MY employees who listen to talk radio—and they are all men of course," she continues, "are the ones who are the angriest."

"Interesting," I say.

Then, with complete distain in her voice but asking as if she was interested in my response (which she wasn't), she asks, "So, why do you HATE so much? Why do you want to spread your hate to so many people?"

I'll come back to the story later, but let's apply this scenario to you. You and I know that when we go to certain functions, there's always going to be "that guy" (or gal) there. The one who is itching for the fight. They've watched CNN or MSNBC, studied Huff Post and the Daily Kos online, and they can't wait to "put you in your place." Why do they do that? I'll explain in a bit.

You have to ask yourself the question: Is the possibility of ruining the evening worth engaging this person? There's a time to fight and a time to walk away. I REALLY don't like engaging people like Senorita Crazy, and it never ends well for them. I also don't enjoy giving them the attention they so desire.

My first move, especially when I'm with family and friends, is to try and defuse the situation. A small, self-deprecating joke or an attempt at changing the mood often works. "You know, I think I remember what day you're talking about. I don't think I was spewing hate, I'm pretty sure I had gas." Yes, a bad joke and a bit crude, but it's something to change the feeling in the room and get people to want the other person to calm down.

When Senorita Crazy asks, "Why do you HATE so much?" My initial reaction is to get angry, but I know it's her goal to piss me off (apologies to my Baptist and LDS friends) and to embarrass me in front of others.

I had dinner with conservative author, Ann Coulter a couple of years ago. She gets a bad rap from the press because she's tough, she tells the truth, and she says things the left HATES. Part of the reason they despise her so much is that her research and writing is so solid you can't beat her on the facts, so they attack her personally.

It really upsets me when she gets so savagely criticized by the left. I think she's incredibly smart, beautiful, and absolutely fearless. If she were spouting commie talking points she would be heralded as a feminist icon up there with Hillary Clinton, Jane Fonda, and Wilma Flintstone.

She has an incredible book on debating liberals called, How to Talk to a Liberal (If You Must): The World According to Ann Coulter

So, I'm at dinner with Ann and a few friends at a restaurant in DC. Somebody brought a guy who nobody else knew, and he REALLY wanted to get involved in our conversation. Well Ann and I have been friends for a long time, we hadn't had a chance to catch up, and this guy keeps trying to interrupt and it wasn't even pertinent to the conversation, he just wanted to talk. We let him ramble on with his nonsense and then got back to our conversation. About 30 minutes in and 3 three drinks later, this guy insists he's going to get in the middle of our business discussion. Ann does something, I had never seen before and it was brilliant at shutting this guy down.

He says, "Hey! I got something to say!" at a very inappropriate time.

Coulter looks at him says in a no uncertain way, "And... I'm done with you."

She turned her face and body away from him, and never acknowledged him again.

It was really funny, super effective, and you knew she meant it!

You might say, "Ann Coulter was being mean to that guy!" No, that guy was rude, pushy and inconsiderate of everyone around. We were talking about serious business issues, and he had no reason to interrupt other than he wanted her attention. She completely cut off her attention to him, and he quietly went away.

There is a time and a place for group conversations, and a time for you to let other people talk. He didn't follow that basic rule. So, Ann Coulter isn't mean - she's really smart.

Had that guy been allowed to take over the conversation, he would have ruined the evening for everyone else. He was drinking heavily and becoming more and more belligerent. She shut him down with one line and obvious body language. Ann Coulter quickly and quietly saved the party for everyone, except "Dan the Drinker" and taught me a great lesson. Clear, obvious body language can be more effective in a moment, than hours of debate. Especially if that person is inebriated, or just doesn't want to listen.

RULE #1

Pick your battles. (P.Y.B.)

Don't fall for the traps.

**Remove your attention from someone
who is being disruptive.**

CHAPTER 2

KEEP FAMILY AND FRIENDS CLOSE

If you can find something everyone agrees on, it's wrong.

— Rep. Mo Udall, D-Ariz.

Now that you know that the goal of the "Looney Lefty" is to get you angry and embarrass you around your family and friends, this is where we quietly and carefully turn things around on them. Just like Ann Coulter did.

The approval of others, in psychological terms, is called, "social proof."

I hate Wikipedia, but they have a pretty good definition: "Social proof is a type of conformity. When a person is in a situation where they are unsure of the correct way to behave, they will often look to others for cues concerning the correct behavior. When "we conform because we believe that others' interpretation of an ambiguous situation is more accurate than ours and will help us choose an appropriate course of action,"[1] it is informational social influence."

There are 5 types of social proof:

1. Expert
2. Celebrity
3. User
4. Wisdom of the crowd
5. Wisdom of your friends

We see social proof around us all the time. When we see commercials of good-looking people having a great time at the beach drinking Coca-Cola, we get the feeling that the sugary drink brings happiness, *(for me it brought Type II diabetes, bada-bing! Hey! Two drink minimum folks!)*. Coke spends millions of dollars a year on advertising, giving the world the social proof that Coke is something that will make you feel better. Look at a few of their slogans over the years:

"Things Go Better with Coca-Cola"

"Can't Beat the Feeling!"

"Life Tastes Good"

"Open Happiness"

"Taste the Feeling"

Each one of those slogans is filled with emotions and good feelings. Social proof, that Coca-Cola will make you *feel good*. (I was going to write, "Coke makes you feel good," then figured some of you "Wisenheimers" would make a drug reference, so I took it out.)

When you see a picture of someone with a celebrity, social proof is implied, and the individual's importance is proven, subconsciously, because they are in a picture with someone we perceive is important.

Rusty Humphries, with the Kardashians, giving social proof that he's the most important person in the world.

Photograph courtesy of Rusty Humphries

Of course, not all social proof ploys work with everyone. Your reaction to my picture with the Kardashian sisters is based on many factors. Are you a fan of theirs? Do you follow them on a regular basis? If so, that picture gives subconscious proof that

I'm valuable simply by proximity. If you have no interest in the Kardashians, that picture might have no impact. If you despise them, a negative impact, and so on.

I know what you're thinking, "What does all of this mean, Rusty?? Why do I care about you and the Kardashians?" Settle down Bucky; I'm getting there!

For our purposes, we will focus on #4 Wisdom of the crowd and #5 Wisdom of your friends. Everyone seeks some approval from family and friends.

People, especially family and friends, are motivated by the behaviors of individuals around them. The best way to get someone to change their behavior is for them to see how people are responding to their words or actions.

If you're not looking for a verbal fight in a social situation, be around other people. Have fun, laugh. When you see the potential assailant come your way, either ignore them or give a minimal acknowledgment. Remember, you are the bigger person, and the proof is that you are with others and everyone is having fun. This is surprisingly effective at shutting down someone looking to cause trouble, as long as you are very subtle about it.

I have found, if someone is looking for a fight in a social situation, they probably have low self-esteem and are looking for ways to make themselves feel more important or influential.

Take that away from them right away. It will make them feel even smaller and, most likely; they will hide in a corner somewhere sucking down large bottles of liquid courage.

If they persist, you want to keep lots of people around you. Why? As I mentioned in the last chapter, the goal of the evildoer is to try to get you mad and try to embarrass you in front of your friends and family. If you stay calm and diffuse the situation, social proof will work in your favor, the crowd will be on your side, and you will win without having to engage.

When Senorita Crazy started shooting her insults at me, I just smiled, got up, and grabbed some pulled pork from the table across the room. It caused her to become angrier; and by my slowly and deliberately walking away from her to get more food (not angrily getting up and storming out the room), she had to raise her voice for me to hear her from the further distance. The combination of these two things made the guests very uncomfortable with her actions. This put me in the position of simultaneously being the victim and, because I had a knowing smile and didn't respond, raised my social status to the authority figure as well.

The group rarely understands why they feel a certain way, but you can control a room with your responses and emotions.

Be prepared to quietly use these techniques. This will keep your family and friends on your side.

RULE #2

Use social proof to your advantage, and stay
close to other people.

Allow the other person to be the bad guy.

No need to verbally fight back.

Be deliberate and subtle.

CHAPTER 3

LEFT VS. RIGHT THOUGHT PROCESSES

To understand the working of American politics, you have to understand this fundamental law: Conservatives think liberals are stupid. Liberals think conservatives are evil.

—Charles Krauthammer, Syndicated Columnist,
Fox News Contributor

One of the reasons there's such a huge divide in America today is because folks on the left and right think differently. Because I'm speaking in broad terms, some generalizations have to be made. In my thousands of hours of interviews and dealings in public, these generalizations are usually accurate.

When I'm writing or speaking, I break down the needs of that particular audience and discern how I can reach them in the best way.

I have found that those on the right tend to think and talk in terms of reason and logic.

I own a business that I love! I get to help people fulfill their dreams. In addition to my top-rated podcast, I am a VIP media talent coach. I help entrepreneurs, corporate executives, actors/actresses, professional speakers and celebrities on radio and television, many of whom you know and admire, be better communicators. Many of my clients are conservative politicians. Between you and me, when I first start working with them, they drive me crazy! Why? Because they think in terms of reason and logic and like to use a lot of big words, throwing out facts and figures using numbers and charts to prove they a right about a subject. In other words, they can be really, really boring.

People on the left tend to think in emotional terms. What feels good, what feels bad... those are what drive the arguments that come from the Left. In almost every topic or subject you can think of, boil down the Democrat response, and you will find it originates from an emotional point of view.

I've been in several Hollywood movies as an actor, and I'm always asked why I think actors and actresses are usually liberals. I believe it goes back to acting classes and living a childlike lifestyle. When you take an acting class, for example, the teacher tells you to lie on the ground and pretend to be an omelet. He has you shaking and popping, trying to get you to feel like an omelet. From a reason and logic point of view, the whole exercise is ludicrous. Of course, you're not an omelet; you're human being trying to learn how to be a good actor. But, what makes a good actor? Is it somebody that knows his or her lines? No, in my experience, the best actors are the ones who can strip away all reason and logic in the mind, and just rely on feeling. (Use the Force, Luke!) You don't honestly think you're an omelet, but you can fool yourself into feeling like one.

Sean Penn is a good actor... and an absolute lunatic, but why? Because he successfully stripped away all his reason and logic and can laser focus on his emotions.

I did an interview with actor Gary Busey a couple of years ago. He was in town to talk about the effects of traumatic brain injury. In 1988, while riding a motorcycle and not wearing a helmet, Busey had an accident that almost killed him, and it left him brain damaged but functional. He's a fascinating guy and was very open with me.

I asked him about his Oscar-nominated role as Buddy Holly in the 1978 film *The Buddy Holly Story*. He told me something that I will never forget. I asked him how he prepared for the role of Buddy Holly, and Busey said, "I wasn't acting in that movie. Buddy Holly took over my body. I was just a vessel for Buddy to tell his story." I have no doubt that in Gary Busey's mind, it felt like Buddy Holly had taken over.

Rusty Humphries providing more social proof with
Gary Busey and his son, actor Jake Busey.

Photograph courtesy of Rusty Humphries

I think that using your heightened state of emotions is great if you are creating art or entertainment, or even working closely with children. But it is not the right mindset if you're trying to run a country as great and powerful as the United States of America.

Here's the rub: liberals use too much emotion, and conservatives don't use enough. Any argument based on emotion is easy to make: "We should allow illegal immigrants to stay because they have families here." The logical response: "They shouldn't have come here in the first place." This reply isn't as compelling or persuasive, especially when you're dealing with people who aren't really into politics that much.

When the time is right, and it's time to fight back, this is when we beat them at their own game.

Saul Alinsky's 1971 book *Rules for Radicals* has been one of the most damaging influences on America since Benedict Arnold. This book, this evil, frickin' book, has inspired more hate, empowered more idiots, and caused more damage than Mrs. O'Leary's cow did when it started the Great Chicago Fire in 1871. The fire Alinsky started decades ago is still burning white hot and has fueled a Grand Canyon-sized divide in this country.

Without going into great detail, Alinsky — a spawn of Satan — taught that the ends justify the means. He thought that lying, cheating, and stealing are okay as long as it furthers the cause.

25

Ridicule people to take away their dignity; thereby, you are destroying their power, and so on. I trace the sharp divide in our country, the fostering of the politics of personal destruction, and the intense hatred being spewed today in the street and online back to this evil, evil man, whom I hope is frying in hell right now.

(Authors note: I don't want to give away too much of my personal opinions in this chapter, so I'm downplaying my thoughts and feelings about Saul Alinsky.)

The verbal weapons available to the Left are few, powerful, but predictable.

They boil down to…

- "You're a racist."

- "You're mean."

And… that's about it.

"President Trump does mean tweets, and he's a racist because he wants to build a wall."

"The NRA is mean because they want people to have guns, and guns kill children."

"The right wing is evil; they don't believe in global warming, so they must hate children, clean water, and fresh air."

A friend of mine, comic and author Even Sayet, breaks down the different thinking patterns in his book *The Kindergarten of Eden. How the Modern Liberal Thinks.*

To paraphrase: People on the right believe that those on the left are stupid. We don't agree with them, but it doesn't mean we hate them. Other the other hand, those on the left see the opinions of the right as evil. In their minds, evil cannot be tolerated, it must be destroyed. Which is what we are seeing in America today.

Below is a transcript of a part of Sayet's speech at The Heritage Foundation featured in Michael Morris' "Evan Sayet: Modern Liberalism's Quest for 'Indiscriminateness' Is a 'Rejection of Thinking,' an 'Utopian Ideology'" (blog), on *cnsnews.com*, March 3, 2017:

> *In the 1980s, thinking was outlawed. It was deemed by the left to be a hate crime. The thinking behind the rejection of thinking is this: anything that you believe, anything that I believe, anything that anybody believes, the people at home believe, anything anybody believes is going to be so tainted by your personal prejudices – prejudices we all have, that we can't help but have just by being human – prejudices like: based on the color of your skin, the nation of your ancestry, your height, your weight, your sex and so-on. Anything that you believe is going to be so tainted by your personal prejudices that the only way not to be a bigot is to never think at all.*

It's actually the second law of the Unified Field Theory of Liberalism that explains why it is, because the purpose of not thinking – it's actually a[n] utopian ideology.

On the one hand, the mindless foot soldiers – those who have been indoctrinated – they believe that if you eliminate thinking, because thinking is an act of bigotry, you can eliminate bigotry. If you eliminate bigotry, the world would be a place where everybody loves one another and Kumbaya.

To the true believers, they are against rational thought. And it was Howard Zinn who said, "Objectivity is impossible." What makes it impossible? Our prejudices. He said, it's also impossible, it's also undesirable.

What makes it undesirable? The true believer is convinced that if we can eliminate the recognition of the better, even the quest for the better, we can eliminate all war. After all, if nothing is better than anything else – if America isn't better than the Soviet Union, if Christianity and Judaism isn't better than Islamism, if nothing is better than anything else – then we would never fight.

If we didn't fight, we wouldn't go to war. Without war there would be none of the poverty that war causes. Without poverty there would be none of the crime that poverty causes. Without crime there would be none of the injustice that crime causes, and we would have this utopian universe.

So the modern liberal was raised to believe that indiscriminateness is a moral imperative because it will bring about paradise.

The problem is it doesn't eliminate prejudice because when everything you need to know you learned in kindergarten – that's the book I meant to refer to just a moment ago – everything you need to know you learned in kindergarten and everything you believe is prejudged. Not only is everything prejudged, it can't be changed by further facts and information because if you don't really need to know anything you learn after kindergarten, then you believe what you believed when you were five years old and nothing could come along –

The bigot can be changed, but the modern liberal cannot be changed. And the idea that by tearing down the good and elevating the evil so everything meets in the middle, so we have nothing to fight about, that doesn't work either. Because the second law of the Unified Field Theory of Liberalism is that indiscriminateness of thought does not lead to indiscriminateness of beliefs.

Indiscriminateness of thought leads invariably and inevitably to the modern liberal siding with evil over good, wrong over right, ugly over beautiful, profane over profound, failure over success. Why? Because if nothing – if no culture, no religion, no form of governance, no familial construct, no behavior – if nothing is better than anything else, then success is unjust.

Why should a person, a culture, a religion, a nation – why should something succeed if it's not better than anything else?

For the same reason, to the modern liberal, failure, as proven by nothing other than the fact that it has failed, failure is in and of itself all the proof that's required that somehow the failure has been victimized.

Why should a person, a culture, a nation – why should something fail if it's not worse than anything else?

For the same reason, just by extension, if success and failure s proof positive of an injustice, then great success and great failure is proof positive of great injustice, and long-sustained success and failure is proof positive of the greatest and most sustained injustices of all.

So, for example, when the modern liberal looks at the Middle East and he sees the nation of Israel, with its miraculous successes – unparalleled in human history the number of Nobel Prize winning scientists they have, and fabulous cities like Tel Aviv and symphony orchestras – well why should they be so successful? They look over at the Palestinians and if there is no difference between Islam and Judaism, then why are the Palestinians so failed?

So it's got to be, not only that Israel is an injustice but that miraculous success, unparalleled successes must be a great injustice, and the same thing on the other side.

And one of the corollaries of the Unified Field Theory of Liberalism is that the modern liberal will ascribe to the innocent exactly the level of evil that he is invariably championing.

How in the world do you look at Israel and say they're genocidal, when the population in the West Bank and the Gaza Strip has been growing? They've been saying for 60 years that Jews are committing this genocide, yet the population of Jews are great and everything else are terrible with genocide.

How do you look at it? It's because the Islamic culture is genocidal.

How does Jimmy Carter look at Israel and say it's an apartheid state when their Islamic, valedictorian is an Islamist? Not Islamist, it is Islamic. There are members of parliament who are Muslim.

How do you look and say they are apartheid? Of course, they're not.

But the modern liberal must elevate the evil they ascribe to the good to exactly the level of evil they are intentionally defending.

Evan Sayet is 100% correct.

When Senorita Crazy attacked me, she started off with comments like,

"You don't understand what it's like to be from the inner city."

"You don't like them because of the color of their skin."

And so on...

Her arguments weren't based in rational thought; they were based on her feelings. She was projecting what she thought I **must** feel because to her, I'm a hater.

The way to take away the arsenal of the Left is to expose their bullying tactics. Call them out; show them right away that you understand their game. Just smile at them; you have their number, and it's funny that they think they can bully YOU.

The Left doesn't want a debate because they don't have the facts to back them up. They want to shut down debate, silence it. They use words like "racist," and "settled science," because they don't want to hear any opposing views.

RULE #3

Study how the other side thinks.

Add emotional elements to your reasonable arguments.

Don't get emotional yourself.

CHAPTER 4

BE THE REASONABLE ONE

Blessed are the peacemakers: for they shall be called the children of God.

—Jesus, *Sermon on the Mount*, Matthew 5:9 KJV

Nobody likes a bully. And if your intention is to either have no political discussion or keep the policy debate at a tolerable level, you always have to be the reasonable one.

I'm not going to put all the blame on the Left — let's be honest. It happens on the right too.

Don't be *one of those guys*. Don't be the jerk looking to cause trouble to prove your point. Nobody likes an ass, and that's why the Democrats chose the donkey as their mascot. They are really good making Asses of themselves. But in a family situation, it's even better if they can make an ass out of you. Don't you be the ass, and don't let "Cousin Gus" make you an ass, either.

Here's a tip that will save your butt many, many times over your life. It's so easy, but so many people refuse to do it.

Listen more than you talk! I can't tell you how important that line is, let me repeat:

Listen more than you talk!

Here's the line I like to use when I'm talking with or debating someone who is yapping on and on incessantly.

"You're either talking… or waiting to talk."

That gets the crowd thinking that maybe the *other* guy IS being rude and obnoxious. It's a good line and worthy for you to remember too. Don't be the person doing all the gabbing.

Once you've got the other guy talking, listen and use the Socratic method. Ask lots and lots of questions, and listen carefully to the answers. If you're really paying attention, you'll find holes in their argument. Then, help them to defeat themselves by their own answers.

When you do respond, be calm, thoughtful, and void of your personal emotions.

Tucker Carlson, host of *Tucker Carlson Tonight* on the Fox News Channel, is an expert at this technique. He does his homework very well. Watch him and you'll see him verbally setting up his opponent for the kill. If I were a liberal, I would never go on that show.

Carlson is smart, and I don't think I've seen him lose a debate. But arrogance and ego go a long way, and these Lefties come on his show because think they are too smart to be defeated by Carlson. I laugh when I see a smug Progressive on Carlson's show. I know the hammer is coming down, and the guest rarely figures it out: until it's too late.

Carlson is a very smart debater; study the way he handles himself. Emulate his style and you will quickly understand the art of the debate.

Another important lesson is, It's ok to say "I don't know." I debated Rachel Maddow and a group of libs at an event at the University of San Francisco. (Gee, I wonder who the crowd was cheering for?) Looking back, the libs I was debating, just made up many of their answers. Because they had the room on their side, it was easy for them to look like they knew what they were talking about. Later, I went back and researched the B.S., and I was right, she made a bunch of it up. Fortunately, I was honest and said, "Hmm, I'd never heard that before." Or "Wow, that's news to me." I was humble enough to not pretend like I knew everything, and they weren't able to send me down a trip of defending, or attacking something that wasn't true.

When debating a worthy opponent, ask for specifics. Don't allow him or her to skate the issue or change the subject. Keep them on point on the specifics of an issue.

A perfect example is from a February 2017 segment, where Tucker Carlson and guest Bill Nye the Science Guy debated the issue of climate change.

Carlson, using the Socratic method, forces Nye to answers specifics where there are none. Here's a partial transcript of the exchange:

Bill Nye:	*The evidence for climate change is overwhelming. We're looking for an explanation that why you guys are having so much trouble.*

Carlson quickly stops Nye's momentum by pointing out his attempt at bullying and condescension.

Tucker Carlson:	*Slow down, before the name-calling begins and before you try to end the conversation, let's start it by asking what exactly you mean. Now, I think most people are open to saying that the climate is changing; it has always changed by the way, as you know.*
Bill Nye:	*It's the rate, Mr. Carlson. It's the rate that's such a concern.*
Tucker Carlson:	*Slow down. The core question from what I can tell is why the change. Is it part of the endless cycle of climate change or is human activity causing it? That seems to be the debate to me and it seems an open question, not a settled question. To what degree human activity is causing that, is it not an open question?*

"Settled science" is the Left's way of ending the discussion. Carlson is setting him up by using Nye's words against him.

Bill Nye:	*It's not an open question; it's a settled question. Human activity is causing climate change.*
Tucker Carlson:	*To what degree?*
Bill Nye:	*To a degree that it's a very serious problem in the next few decades.*
Tucker Carlson:	*No, no, but wait. Stop, stop, stop. You said it's a settled point, and I'm asking a precise question.*
Bill Nye:	*Science knew it's a settled point.*

Carlson asks for specifics. By spouting talking points, you don't have to know the subject all that well. Also, now might have been a good time to say, "Yes, it's settled science, but we are still learning and seeking answers." But he didn't, he had to show that he knew it all. Nye is used to performing for adoring fans that fall into line and believe whatever he tells them. They don't question him or his theories, but when he's asked the tough questions, his arguments fall apart.

Tucker Carlson:	*If you'll listen to me I'll be grateful. To what degree is climate change caused by human activity? Is 100% of climate change caused*

39

by human activity, is it 74.3%? It's settled science, please tell us to what degree human activity is responsible.

Bill Nye: *The word degree is a word that you chose. But the speed that climate change is happening, is caused by humans.*

Tucker Carlson: *Hold on, hold on. To what extent is human activity responsible for speeding that up? I mean, please be more precise.*

Carlson sees Nye getting uncomfortable and he won't allow him to change the subject.

Bill Nye: *If that's the number you want. Humans are causing it to happen catastrophically fast.*

Tucker Carlson: *Okay, at what rate would it have changed without human activity? You look annoyed that I'm asking these questions but they're very basic questions. They're not denial.*

Here, Carlson points out Nye's discomfort, that he "looks annoyed." This takes Nye off his talking points, and his emotions (fear) start to get the better of him.

Bill Nye: *Basically, the cycles of climate change, the last ice age we had was tens of thousands of years ago. Now here's the thing, half the people in*

	the world live on sea coasts. The people live on the sea coasts are going to be displaced.
Tucker Carlson:	You're changing ... you're not answering my question.
Bill Nye:	They are going to be displaced!
Tucker Carlson:	Hold on. I'm asking you a simple question about the rate of climate change. Look, here's the point that I hope our viewers can understand. I'm not in any way denying that the climate is changing. I'm utterly open to the possibility that the change is caused by man's activity. I'm merely calling into question your claim that all of this is settled, that we know precisely what is happening and why. That anyone who asks pointed questions about it is a denier and ought to be imprisoned or shouted off the stage.
Bill Nye:	That was your word. That's not my claim, and I really ...
Tucker Carlson:	Would you like me to read your quote? That people who disagree with you ought to potentially go to jail? You said that.

Bill Nye interview by Tucker Carlson, *Tucker Carlson Tonight*, Fox News Channel, February 2017.

And with that, Nye lost the debate and was humiliated on live national TV. In the past, Nye really has said that people who don't agree absolutely with the theory of climate change, possibly should be jailed.

On April 14, 2016, *The Washington Times* wrote, "Bill Nye, the science guy, is open to criminal charges and jail time for climate change dissenters":

"Asked about the heated rhetoric surrounding the climate change debate, such as Robert F. Kennedy Jr.'s previous comments that some climate skeptics should be prosecuted as war criminals, Mr. Nye replied, "We'll see what happens."

"Was it appropriate to jail the guys from Enron?" Mr. Nye asked in a video interview with Climate Depot's Marc Morano. "We'll see what happens. Was it appropriate to jail people from the cigarette industry who insisted that this addictive product was not addictive, and so on?"

"In these cases, for me, as a taxpayer and voter, the introduction of this extreme doubt about climate change is affecting my quality of life as a public citizen," Mr. Nye said. "So I can see where people are very concerned about this, and they're pursuing criminal investigations as well as engaging in discussions like this."

"Mr. Nye's comments come with a coalition of liberal attorneys general pursuing companies that challenge the consensus of catastrophic climate change. Critics fear the campaign could chill research and free speech."

Let's get back to my story... At this point in the evening, Senorita Crazy decides to take me on directly. As most Lefties do, she starts off by trying to belittle and bully.

"I've traveled the world. I have been to so many countries, I couldn't even count them if I wanted to," she says with her nose stuck so high in the air that I can see a booger snarled in her long, nasty nose hairs.

"The rest of the world is so much smarter than Americans. They know more about the world, they know multiple languages, they embrace diversity, and they know more about America than Americans do. Did you know most American's don't even have a passport? Everyone else around the world has a passport, except us stupid, selfish Americans."

I say, "Did it ever occur to you that maybe America is so big that we don't need to speak multiple languages, and we're so powerful that the world needs to know about us, more than we need to know about them? I'm not saying it's not a good idea to keep up on world events or travel. But, I don't need to spend my days studying the political landscape of Chad to prove to you that I'm smart, or do I?"

"I think it's people like you, who have closed minds and only think America is great. What about other countries, can't they be great too?"

"I wish they would step up and make their countries great, then maybe we wouldn't have to take care of them by sending them our hard-earned money, defending their lands with the blood of our soldiers, and then paying for their defenses for generations. Yes! I do think America is that great! And, I'm damn proud of my country. My father fought and died for our country, so believe me, I understand the sacrifices made. But, listen here honey (throwing in a little dig, tee-hee), no country in the history of the world has done more to feed to poor, heal the sick, and protect the innocent than America!"

She snarls at my "honey" comment and hisses back, trying to take control of the situation. "We can agree to disagree. But, you have to agree that the people of the world are much smarter than most Americans."

(Now I start asking questions)

"Hmmm, that's very interesting, why do you think that is?" I asked.

"Because they watch more news, read, and study documentaries much more than American's do," she stated. "They don't just obsess on Fox News."

(Asking for specifics)

Replying in a calm voice, "It's true. News organizations like the BBC, while I think they are biased, do have in-depth reporting. What sources do you like, or what do you think the people around the world rely on for news about the USA?"

And she says... "I love NPR, MSNBC is the only honest cable network, and I think Michael Moore is a genius, and all the people I talk to around the world think he's one of the most honest men on the planet."

I choke on my drink as I spit it out of my mouth. I'm hoping I won't die from the liquid running down my windpipe before I put this moron in her place. I let loose an uncontrollable belly laugh! I think to myself—GAME ON! She's just lost, big time!

"Fascinating, Michael Moore is the worlds most honest man? I'd never heard that before." I nonchalantly go to my cell phone and type in "probable Michael Moore lies," and in an instant, up pops numerous hits. I don't look for an article written by a conservative; I want something from the far Left. It needs to be clear, unquestionable, and powerful.

And then...

(Cue the music of 1,000 angels.)

(VOICEOVER—Rusty like Moses—seeing the Promised Land for the first time)

The Lord answered my prayers. Appearing from the glow of my magical iPhone was the perfect debating weapon. The great Oracle, also known as the all-knowing and all-powerful "Google," called me to the mountaintop to bestow upon me the ultimate gift.

Behold... a glorious article that had everything needed to prove Senorita Crazy's ridiculousness!

Published by *Slate Magazine*, a proud left-wing rag, was "Unfairenheit 9/11 The Lies of Michael Moore," by Christopher Hitchens, June 21, 2004.

If you don't know this guy Hitchens, he was a real piece of garbage. Before he passed away in 2011, he spent much of his wretched life attacking America and took great pleasure in mocking God.

He was a cult hero to the drug-loving Left, and I'm willing to bet Senorita Crazy spent hours in the dorm, dropping dope, dancing to Dylan, and discussing Hitchens.

I read passages aloud, each one dutifully destroying Michael Moore's credibility. And worse for her, it wasn't me — the big bad conservative who was supposedly "inventing these lies." They were all written her hero, Christopher Hitchens.

With his combination of being a far left-wing jackass AND his years raised high on a progressive pedestal, Senorita Crazy's mind was whiplashed.

Mentally, it was like she was on the freeway behind the wheel of a beautiful little red Smart Car, when a trucker hopped-up on speed and liquor rolled over her at 85 mph, smashing her mind flatter than Wile E. Coyote after the Road Runner fooled him again.

I passionately read what Hitchens wrote:

"To describe this film as dishonest and demagogic would almost be to promote those terms to the level of respectability. To describe this film as a piece of crap would be to run the risk of a discourse that would never again rise above the excremental. To describe it as an exercise in facile crowd-pleasing would be too obvious. Fahrenheit 9/11 is a sinister exercise in moral frivolity, crudely disguised as an exercise in seriousness. It is also a spectacle of abject political cowardice masking itself as a demonstration of 'dissenting' bravery."

"But, but, but..." As she starts to argue, I remind her that Ann Coulter didn't write this column. This is the great, Leftist Christopher Hitchens.

I continue:

"Moore's affected and ostentatious concern for black America is one of the most suspect ingredients of his pitch package. In a recent interview, he yelled that if the hijacked civilians of 9/11 had been black, they would have fought back, unlike the stupid and presumably cowardly white men and women (and children). Never mind for now how many black passengers were on those planes—we happen to know what Moore does not care to mention: that Todd Beamer and a few of his co-passengers, shouting 'Let's roll,' rammed the hijackers with a trolley, fought them tooth and nail, and helped bring down a United Airlines plane, in Pennsylvania, that was speeding toward either the White House or the Capitol. There are no words for real, impromptu bravery like that, which helped save our republic from worse than actually befell. The Pennsylvania drama also reminds one of the self-evident fact that this war is not fought only 'overseas' or in uniform, but is being brought to our cities. Yet Moore is a silly and shady man who does not recognize courage of any sort even when he sees it because he cannot summon it in himself. To him, easy applause, in front of credulous audiences, is everything."

As each word gleefully rolls off my golden tongue, I watch as Senorita Crazy's face turns red. Her eyes squint furiously praying to a god she doesn't believe in, to strike me down quickly and painfully. Her blood boils hot and full of rage.

Right before my eyes I watch this grown woman regressing to a temper tantrum befitting bad elementary school behavior. I imagine she's a giant Pez dispenser about to blow her top and spit a fruity candy treat out of her neck as a present. I giggle to myself, just a little.

The people in the group, who weren't very political to begin with, begin to see her arguments fall apart and her anger grow. This causes her to escalate the fight further. She has let her emotions take full control of her thoughts and actions. The transformation is obvious, it's physical, it's in my face, and I'm ready. Hell hath no fury like a woman scorned!

Never forget, facts never stop a liberal because a liberal never learns from lessons learned.

So-called Progressives have an answer for everything, and everything has the same answer. Grow government bigger, another law will solve all your problems, and you can never spend enough government money, ever.

No matter how many times these solutions fail, they always go back to the same faulty and expensive mistakes. The American Left of 2017, is the definition of insanity. Doing the same thing over and over and expecting different results.

RULE #4

Act calm, cool, and collected.

Be polite.

Listen more than you talk.

Ask a lot of questions. (Socratic method)

Okay to say "I don't know."

Be the bigger person; it makes them look even worse.

CHAPTER 5

ENGAGE AND BE ENGAGING

Let's Get It On!

— Judge Mills Lane, Legendary Boxing Referee

Persuasion is a two-edged sword - reason and emotion, plunge it deep.

— Dr. Lew Sarett, Organic chemist, first to synthesize cortisone 1917 – 1999

It has come down to this: the Lefty at the party won't leave you alone. They have continued to say stupid things, which you know are outright lies or just plain wrong, and you can no longer sit by and allow this jerk to go unanswered.

First, make sure you haven't allowed your emotions to take over. As hard as it may be, this is very important: YOU MUST STAY IN CONTROL OF YOUR EMOTIONS! If you lose it, you may lose the argument but most importantly, you risk the respect of your family and friends. Remember why you got this book: you want to KEEP your family and friends. I'm not saying you need to back off or stand down. But you need to be smart, savvy, and ready. By allowing your opponent to push your buttons, it's next to impossible to keep your reason and logic intact.

I've known conservative author Ben Shapiro since he was 16 years old. As a high school kid, he would send me columns he had written that read as if he were a 40-year-old political scientist. His writing, even at that young age, was brilliant. I'm so proud to see how far his career is going within the conservative movement and beyond.

If you want to delve even deeper into this topic of debating Leftists, Shapiro has written two outstanding books, *How to Debate Leftists and Destroy Them: 11 Rules for Winning the Argument* and *Bullies: How the Left's Culture of Fear and Intimidation Silences Americans.*

Shapiro proved his mastery of this subject in an interview he did with Pierce Morgan, formerly of CNN. Shapiro pointed out that in the wake of the ghastly December 14, 2012, Sandy Hook Elementary massacre, Morgan had made himself the face of the gun control movement. Shapiro noticed that Morgan always called his opponents racist. From *How to Debate Leftists and Destroy Them: 11 Rules for Winning the Argument* Shapiro wrote:

"Morgan would bring on folks from the right and then suggesting they were evil for disagreeing with him. Or, alternatively, he brings on kooks like Alex Jones, wait for them to go berserk, and then suggested all gun owners were berserk nuts waiting to go off. When he had on Larry Pratt of Gun Owners of America, he called him an "Unbelievably stupid man" after Pratt pointed out gun control's failure in municipalities across the country. He then added, "You have absolutely no coherent argument, you don't actually give a damn about the gun murder rate in America."

Piers Morgan – Liberal Bully Ben Shapiro - Author
Photograph courtesy of CNN

Within a few days, Shapiro was asked to be on *Piers Morgan Live* to discuss his disagreements with the way Morgan handled his interviews.

SHAPIRO: *"You know, honestly Piers, you have kind of been a bully on this issue, because what you do, and I've seen it repeatedly on your show. What you tend to do is you demonize people who differ from you politically by standing on the graves of the children of Sandy Hook saying*

*they don't seem to care enough about dead kids.
If they cared more about the dead kids, they
would agree with you on policy. I think we can
have a rational, political conversation about
these balancing rights and risks and rewards of
all of these different policies, but I don't think
that we need to do is demonize other people on
the other side is being unfeeling about what
happened at Sandy Hook."*

Shapiro took the fight right to Piers before the boring Brit had a chance to pounce.

Next, Shapiro, in a brilliant move, continued to paint Morgan as a bully. Remember social proof? Group think? Using emotion? By not falling into the trap of allowing Morgan to call him a bully, Shapiro was able to turn the tables, win the debate, and watch his career skyrocket.

Schapiro wrote, "Later on in the interview, Piers would come back to this point belittling me personally because he disagreed with my arguments on Second Amendment rights. Again, I hammer home the point that Piers was a loudmouth and a bully."

MORGAN: *Do you know how absurd you sound?*

SHAPIRO: *Here's where you going to the "absurd" and
the "bullying." "You're absurd, you're stupid." I understand –*

MORGAN: *I'm not bullying.*

SHAPIRO: *Of course you are.*

MORGAN: *I'm not the one who came in here and accused you of standing on the graves of dead children.*

SHAPIRO   *Because you're the one who's doing that. I'm punching bag twice as hard.*

MORGAN: *That's what I call bullying.*

SHAPIRO: *You know when I call it? Punching back twice as hard, in the words of President Obama.*

MORGAN: *That's what I call bullying.*

SHAPIRO: *This is astonishing.*

MORGAN: *What's astonishing?*

SHAPIRO: *What's astonishing about it is for weeks now, you have been saying that anyone who disagrees with your position is absurd, idiotic, and doesn't care about the dead kids in Sandy Hook. And that when I say that it's a bullying tactic, you turn around and say that I'm bullying you for saying that. It's absurd. It's ridiculous.*

Watch and learn from a master in an unfriendly environment. Ben Shapiro interview by Piers Morgan, *Piers Morgan Live,* CNN, January 10, 2013.

After I read a few "Michael Moore is a big, fat liar" quotes, Senorita Crazy goes into full-on attack mode.

She screams at the top of her lungs.

"You're just a hater!"

Angry babies from miles around feel jealous of her sheer screaming supremacy. She has completely lost it now.

"It's people like you who are running everything! You put your hate on the radio and teach others to hate too! You hate women, minorities, immigrants, and LGBTQ people! Why do you hate someone because of who they love? Why do you hate everyone! You are directly responsible for the hate that MY men feel at work and at home! They are probably beating their wives and children because of you! Because of the hate you give them permission to have! The only thing they love is hate!

"It's you, Rush Limbaugh, Sean Hannity, and your evil radio shows that are tearing our country apart! IT'S AAAALLLLL YOOOOOOOUUURRRRREEEE FFFAAAAALLLUUUUTTTT!!!"

RULE #5

Disarm the bully quickly.

Don't allow him to strike first.

Allow the other person to lose control of their emotions.

CHAPTER 6

IT'S OKAY (TO APPEAR) TO LOSE

Nothing proves more persuasive than a clearly stated fact.

—Donald Rumsfeld, *Rumsfeld's Rules*, congressman, President Gerald R. Ford's Chief of Staff, the youngest AND oldest U.S. Secretary of Defense

I want to make something crystal clear. Just because someone is a Democrat, doesn't mean they are a bad person. There are millions of wonderful people who relate to the ideas that the Democratic Party espouses. That's ok and I respect that. Those are the people I want to talk with. It's the politicians and those that profit by the great American divide that are unreachable. An honest man or woman, who spends more time with their job and kids than they do with Drudge, CNN or Fox News can be easily misguided by the news they hear, but they are reachable. Treat them with respect; speak with reason, logic and emotion. You can persuade them. Be kind, understanding and most importantly be patient with them. Those are not the folks we have been focusing on in this book.

I really enjoy an honest political debate. I do. A lot of times I will come into a room at a get together and someone will say,

"We're not talking politics here today." I smile because I know one of these people is probably looking for a political fight. I know it's coming and I'm prepared.

I always nod, smile, and agree with the host. I'm not there to fight. I'm not there to debate. I'm not there to do my radio show. I'm not there to defend Rush Limbaugh or President Trump. I'm there to spend time with family and friends. But, I know it's coming. It usually takes about 30 minutes for somebody to nonchalantly come up and say something political. If the host sees this conversation and says lightheartedly, "I said no politics," I say in an amicable tone, "It's okay, I love to have open discussions with people, whether they agree with me or not."

And then I listen and listen and smile and nod. I'm always positive, confident in what I believe, and willing to hear to their point of view. This tactic almost always defuses any social situation. I let the person say their piece, and I nod as if I'm interested in their opinion. Usually, it's some talking point they saw online, or a news story they misunderstood. I may gently point out a few discrepancies in what they said and let them know the truth of what happened.

My response is soft, respectful, and enlightened unless they are outright lying, disrespectful, or on the attack.

I'm always mindful of the host or hostess. I'm sure they are mentally freaking out thinking, "Oh no, these guys are going to ruin my party!" I don't blame them; I never want to ruin someone's event. I appreciate that they were kind enough to invite me.

So, I smile. I smile at the host. I smile at the person I'm having the discussion with. I smile and nod, smile and nod, smile and nod. This should be all it takes to keep the evening on course.

However, should the other person take it up a notch, that's when you must decide how important it is, and does it need to escalate?

I ALWAYS try to keep things cool... always. One way to end things is to say, "I gotta go to the bathroom. Let's pick this up later." Smile, walk away, and never come back to the dude. He might be frustrated, or he may think he just won the argument. Do you care? Is it worth ruining a party because some guy is a jerk? Do *you* want to be the jerk that escalated it? Or do you want to be the *respectful* one that ended it?

Be aware of the room and the situation. Keep social proof on your side, even if they are a group of liberals. Be the reasonable person. It's okay to agree with little points made by liberals:

LIBERAL: Republicans in Congress suck.

YOU (calmly): I agree, but I'll add one thing, BOTH parties in Congress suck! That's why we elected Donald Trump. You may think he's mean because of his tweets and racist

because he wants to protect our border.
But, try to think of it this way: Why do
BOTH parties hate President Trump? It's
not because of the tweets or the border
or Russia or any of the garbage they are
pushing in the media right now. It's
because he wants to disrupt the power
in D.C. Both parties want money and
power. We put President Trump in to try
and stop the growth of bad government
and the supremacy of the elites. You
might call those people the 1%ers, and
they are on both sides of the aisle. Diane
Feinstein, Nancy Pelosi, Darrell Issa.
These are some of the richest people in the
world. How do you get in Congress and
wind up with 30 million dollars or more?
That's not right, Democrat or Republican.
Some members of Congress earned that
wealth and had it before they got into
government, but others? You tell me
how they got rich? I just feel it's time to
stop fighting each other. It's time to focus
on those jerks who are spending all our
money on stupid stuff and getting rich
while doing it.

That is a fair and honest reply. Give an answer like that, with feeling and kindness in your voice, displaying no anger (unless your ire is aimed at members of both parties). Most of the time, that's all a Liberal wants to hear, and that is that. If you ask me, that's a solid win.

The other scenario: you get drawn into a fight. Let's be honest. If you engage with the idiot and it heats up and there's a big fight and you win, are they going to give you a new car? Of course not. So, where is the victory? You want to be the tough guy and show how smart you are? That never ends as well as you imagine it will.

I rarely fight with these idiots, and I end it if it starts to escalate. It doesn't bother me if they think they "beat" me. I know I won because I didn't allow them to ruin someone else's pleasant evening. They can walk around all night thinking that they're a badass, "I took on the talk show host!" I know better, and you should too.

By now, Senorita Crazy is to the point where I'm thinking about calling the cops. She screaming uncontrollably and looks like she's going to hurt herself. I know she wants to kill me. But, how do I get it to end?

RULE #6

It's not cool to ruin someone else's party.

Smile and nod.

**Give them a small victory if you need to;
it's no big deal.**

End the escalation! (You win)

CHAPTER 7

CONCLUSION

If someone doesn't want to believe the truth, there's nothing you can do to change his or her mind.

— Rusty Humphries Very attractive broadcasting and media genius, author, singer, dancer, dreamer 1965 - 2075

It's a lot easier to write, "End the escalation and walk away," than it is when the situation has become heated and frustrating... Believe me my brother sister, I understand.

It should be okay to talk politics and religion in mixed company. It just needs to be done delicately, without the intent of trying to hurt somebody or change his or her mind. In today's environment, you're probably not going to be able to do that. Know that going in. If you can politely talk in mixed company, agree to disagree and enjoy the evening. Everyone goes home happy. That's the win! That's what I want for you.

I should have taken my own advice when dealing with Senorita Crazy, but she pushed me too far. By accusing me of hate speech on the radio and insinuating I was ruining the lives of her male employees and everyone else across America, I allowed my emotions to take over, and I responded, **hard**. I used her "Michael Moore is the "World's most honest man," comment and methodically tore apart every argument, shallow thought, and emotional response in her weak arsenal.

I didn't know it at the time, but Senorita Crazy is an Alpha woman who is used to weak people submitting to her every word, or she verbally beats them down. She couldn't do that with me, and it hurt her. My guess is that she suffers from *narcissistic personality disorder*. *Psychology Today* magazine describes it like this:

> *"A person whose grandiosity soars to such heights that they are manipulative and easily angered, especially when they don't receive the attention they consider their birthright."*

I describe it as "one of those people who think the world revolves around them." Clinton, Obama, and Trump all share this disorder and I'm sure you have people in your life that do too.

I have found that the MOST important thing to a narcissist is... their perceived reputation. If they think the world and everyone revolves around them, and something makes them look bad, their world falls apart. If you believe your opponent is a narcissist, take them down a peg or two, and you will be shocked at how quickly they destruct.

(Cue Rusty doing a bad Howard Cosell impression as the announcer – Cue Rusty admitting he's an old guy because he just referenced Howard Cosell.)

It's the Final Round (Ding-ding) — I have her on the ropes. Her college-commie-buddies-approved Michael Moore argument has landed no blows and has the unintended consequence of being proven false by a conservative, reading a liberal publication aloud.

Senorita Crazy is backed into the corner and has nowhere to go but an all-out, emotional, verbal, nuclear assault on me. And, had I not been equipped with the inside secrets of the Left's weak debate playbook, she would have been able to distract and confuse me. (End bad Cosell impression)

Try to follow her logic.

(If you can't, don't worry because you're sane.)

"When I was in high school, I lived in a very rich, white, suburban neighborhood."

(nearly in tears, apologizing for her "white privilege")

"Thankfully, I was bused across town to an all-black school during desegregation."

(with great pride, touting her superiority)

"They are MY people! You don't understand, MY people!"

(Arrogantly, attempting to prove that I'm a racist and she is of grander stature because of her great concern for diversity and

people of color. Where I, of course, must hate everyone wh
isn't white.)

By the way, at no point did the subject of race or color ever com
up… not until she launched into her outbreak. Remember, t
the Left, the ultimate insult is you are a racist; it's the ultimat
sin. NEVER take the bait, ever! Memorize this, nod and smile
nod and smile, nod and smile.

I stood back and let her rant. Oh, my friend, what a rant it was
For the next 20 minutes, she flailed her arms, beat her ches
and yelled in my face with a screech so loud, so accusatory, s
angry, and so full of lies, hate, superiority, and self-righteous
ness. It was as if Hillary Clinton and Elizabeth Warren ha
hatched a spoiled spawn of their own, and I was the recipier
of her laser-focused hate, stanky breath, and spittle! (Yes, I sai
STANKY breath!)

She never once asked me a question. She never took time t
listen to a different point of view. She completely allowed he
emotions to take over. By doing so, she horrified everyone i
about a 2-square mile area.

She shot venom at me like a dragon spits fire. She used all he
tools, her expensive university education, hours of listenin
to NPR and PBS. She faithfully repeated every talking poin
word for word. She performed well. As well as any faithf
Comrade should. And, when she was done, she was done.
she was emotionally spent.

When she looked up, tears were streaming down her cheeks, and her mascara was smudged like a chubby raccoon. She expected to see the crowd on her side. She was ready to be welcomed the victor with hugs, kisses and tears. She played the professional victim card with the skill of a brain surgeon.

I took a deep breath, and calmly said, "Are you ok now?"

Senorita Crazy glared, wiping the tears from her victimized eyes.

Calmly I begin, "Had you asked, I would have agreed with you that Congress sucks, on both sides."

Now I start to empathize with her.

"I have to say, I'm so impressed with your stories. The way you live your life only looking out of the little guy. You never ever do anything for yourself, am I right?"

"No, I don't do anything for myself. It's so hard sometimes. Nobody understands me," she whines.

I say, "The world is a better place because of people like you. You altruistically place the needs of everyone else above any desires you may have emotionally or materialistically. I mean, am I right?"

She sniffs and nods like a child who is being forgiven for bad behavior.

"It's hard to find someone so caring and noble, a person so generous," I coo as I set her up for the kill. "You would rather die than you put your wants before the needs of others. Right?"

"Yes..." in a tone that says "someone finally understands me."

In my head, I'm ready for this to end. One more line and the evening's over. Looking at the driveway, I say, "Hey, that's a sweet Mercedes AMG you have there. What does something like that cost, about $125,000? Thank the Lord, you're looking out for the little guy!" With a couple of short sentences, I shattered the tension and exposed her hypocrisy. The crowd at the party uncontrollably broke out laughing. It was quick and easy, for me.

For Senorita Crazy, it was devastating. When I was done, it broke her. It did, I took it too far.

She came to the party with the mission of destroying me, her perceived enemy. Instead, she left with her friends laughing at her, tears running down her face, crying, "Everyone here is against me!" She ran off crying, realizing what a capitalistic pig she was driving off in her sweet $125,000 Mercedes.

I wasn't profane, mean, abusive, or aggressive in any way, but I annihilated her core beliefs. And, I'm not sure she has recovered.

It wasn't just because of this incident, but she has since moved out of the country and now has minimal contact with her circle of friends.

The host couple agreed that I had handled it correctly and said it was she who was the aggressor. They thought she deserved it. But, I haven't spent any time with my old friends since, and I fear that long relationship is probably over.

Senorita Crazy had some serious issues before she walked into dinner delivering a single flower for each of us. I thought she was a little weird right away, but I allowed her to get under my skin.

She acted like she was ready to "rumble," but I should have known better, and I should have stopped her escalation of the situation.

I regret that evening to this day.

Learn from my lesson.

A fun, fiery, good-natured debate is great, but a knock down political war, with family and friends around, isn't worth it. It isn't.

Real strength knows when to let the other guy *feel* like he has won a battle of no consequence.

RULE #7

Your family and friends are more important than an unimportant fight.

Be smart, kind, and generous with your patience.

Not everyone who disagrees with you is a bad person.

Go home happy, with your family and friends intact.

Follow these rules and...

You win!

ABOUT THE AUTHOR

Rusty Humphries is a 37-year veteran of the radio and TV industry.

Starting as a high schooler hired to clean the parking lot of a radio station, Humphries quickly moved up the ladder as a copywriter, DJ, sports reporter, comedy writer, political analyst, and eventually the host of his own nationally syndicated radio talk show. *The Rusty Humphries Show* reached the 6th largest listening audience in the U.S., according to *Talkers Magazine*.

His podcast, *The Rusty Humphries Rebellion* is one of the world's most popular podcasts on politics and pop-culture.

A dynamic speaker and personality, he has appeared on nearly all national broadcast and cable outlets including Fox News Channel, NBC, ABC, CBS, CNN, MSNBC, RT, and many others.

Humphries has broadcast from war zones in Iraq and Afghanistan, interviewed Palestinian terrorists, and traveled to the detention facility at Guantanamo Bay. He has helped in relief efforts in Sudan, Darfur and Cambodia, and has been banned for life from Parliament in the U.K. for asking tough questions to a politician, who didn't like it very much.

His exploits have been fodder for books, TV and radio shows and have even been fictionalized by multi-award winning best-selling author Orson Scott Card in the book "Hidden Empire."

Called **"America's Media Talent Coach,"** Humphries is an expert in broadcasting, business, and VIP talent development. H is CEO of a thriving consulting agency.

Be the "Go-To" Celebrity in your niche market!
"America's Media Talent Coach" Rusty Humphries
has limited openings for VIP Coaching programs.
Find out more at www.RustyLive.com.

Find out more about Rusty Humphries at
RustyLive.com.

The Rusty Humphries Rebellion is available on
iTunes, iHeartRadio, and Stitcher.

Please LIKE and follow on Facebook
https://www.facebook.com/Talk2Rusty/
and @Talk2Rusty on Twitter.

23821313R00054

Printed in Poland
by Amazon Fulfillment
Poland Sp. z o.o., Wrocław